Nunowa: A Corn F￢

And The Storytelling Necklace

BY: Donna Gentle Spirit Barron

PREFIX

Hakame, my name is Donna Barron,
I am an Eastern Woodland Indian of the Matinecock
and Montaukett tribes. My ancestors have lived upon the
North Shores and as far as Montauk Point since time
immemorial.
My Native Spirit Name is Manitou Yohkayut (Gentle Spirit)
Which means, "The Soul of the East Wind". I am required
To defend my own and my family's honor and I pledged
Allegiance to the old ways of our ancestors. My name is
Known to the four winds, I carry a tomahawk as a reminder
Of Warriors who died defending the oath of the old ways.

I share with you one of our traditions
That has been passed down from generation to generation.
It is called Nunowa, a Harvest Ceremony and the Story Telling
Necklace. The Children participate in making the story necklaces
With the Grandmothers. This was a great help to the Mothers,
For it kept the children from being under foot while they
Prepared the feast.

I do enjoy sharing my storytelling with the children.
I am the storyteller of life for my people. It is a role
I was born into and have been sharing it for the last

Seventeen years. Today I use pony beads to tell my

Stories. But I do love to share the traditional Indian Corn,

Pumpkin and squash seeds as a beautiful craft with the children.

Foreword

Donna is a good friend of mine, she has
been for a number of years. She is an Author of
four previous books which I have read. I have become
a fan of her research and writings.

She possesses a fierce love and pride for her heritage.
I know she is the storyteller of life. She holds strongly
To the true history of her ancestors. Her heart, her spirit
Is dedicated to sharing the true history of her ancestors
With the young. For Donna wants to keep the true history
Of her people alive. So this book which she written for
The younger generation, is about her ancestor's celebrations
And traditions, which she hopes the next generation will also
Celebrate and continue to pass on.

Donna writes with truth, love and much pride.
This is a good read for young and old to enjoy and learn.
May Donna continue to tell her stories and keep her
History alive with the future generations to come!

Orlando Roman Hoed Jr.

Author: "The Long Lost Hoed D'beche's

Of Guanabacoa, Cuba"

DEDICATION

The children are our future. They shall

Carry on our traditions. So

I dedicate this book, my story to,

My Great Niece River Josephine Streb.

She, the next future Author in the family.

You are blessed Miss River, Keep on writing!

"Indian Children"

Where we walk to school each day

Indian children used to play –

All about our Native land

Where all the shops and houses stand

And the trees were very tall and

There were no streets at all

Not a church and not a steeple

Only woods and Indian people

Only wigwams on the ground,

And at nights

Bears prowling round

What a different place today

Where we live and work and play!

By: Annette Wynne

1919

CHAPTER ONE

"Tatoson""

There once was a young boy whose name was Tatoson.
He was of the Turtle Clan born here upon Little Neck Bay.
Tatoson resided by the bay with his Mother, Wunnetunia,
His Father, Nuckqusha, three sisters, Qunneke, Aunan and
Weekan and his three brothers, Cowenaweke, Mishquock,
And Wauo`mpeg. Also living upon the bay were his two
Favorite Uncles, Mapevanisto and Cowauontam.

At sunrise each day Tatoson watched as his Uncles
Left for the bay. They were Shell Fishermen. Tatoson
Constantly dreamed of the day when he would be old
enough to go fishing with his Uncles on Little Neck Bay.
As Tatoson went about with his chores of the day
His mind wandered back to the bay. While gathering wood
For the fire, he pictured himself walking through the
woods, passed the brush and saplings until he came to the
Clearing and he could see the bay for miles. His Grandmother
Interrupted his thoughts "Tatoson!" She called,
"go collect the clams' left by the tide on the bay's shore.

Bring them here and put them before the fire." Tatoson
was so excited he dropped his wood for the fire and as a smile
grew on his face he ran to the bay's shore. He hoped to see
his Uncles, maybe raking oysters from the bottom of the bay!
Tatoson could picture the bay just as his Uncles had described
It at sunrise. The dawning sun coming up behind the bay as it lit
up the green marsh. Shell fish in abundance.

The bay so rich in fish and waterfowl. His thoughts were
broken when he came upon his Uncle's campsite along
The bay. Here is where they set up for the day, to harvest
clams and oysters.

Tatoson waded through the inlet and started digging
in the sand with his feet just like his Uncles had taught him.
Bringing the clams up from the bay's floor.

He looked out onto the bay and could make out
his Uncles in the distance. He could see them raking the
bottom of the bay.

Tatoson's mind wandered again, this time picturing
himself grown, rowing out upon the falling tide with his Uncles.
As his thoughts returned back to the water's edge, a smile
came upon Tatosons' face, how he wished to be out on the bay
with his Uncles, but until that day comes when he can row out

onto the bay with tong in hand, he is happy and content to be right here on the water's edge wading and gathering quahog that was left by the tide.

Tatoson knew that next Summer he would be old enough to start Shell fishing with his Uncles. Besides he was so excited for things to come!

Fall season was vastly approaching. Soon they would be returning to their village after the Harvest. The Elders were planning a reunion, Tatoson loved the fall feast! It is called Nunowa, which means Corn Festival and he just could not wait!

Tatoson took one long last look at his Uncles raking the Bottom of the bay before gathering up his Little Neck Clams that he had Collected along the bay's edge.

Grandmother will have these on the fire before sunset, when His Uncles return from a long day of shell fishing.

Tatoson enjoyed spending his days on the water's edge when Grandmother allowed. Today was a good day he thought. tonight with sleep, comes happy dreams of Nunowa.

CHAPTER TWO

"Nunowa"

Nunowa is a coastal Algonquin word which means Corn Festival. Tatoson remembers celebrating Nunowa with his family ever since he was a baby. It is always held in the mid-month of October. Nunowa has been celebrated by Tatosons' Ancestors for thousands of years.

Tatoson and his family are an Eastern Woodland People and All the Wolf, Turtle, and Turkey clans would gather to give thanks to Mother Earth for her bountiful harvest.

It was finally Nunowa and Tatoson was so excited! Soon all his Siblings, Cousins, Grandparents, Aunts & Uncles, everyone will be gathering to enjoy Nunowa.

Tatosons' Mother, Wunnetunia a strikingly tall beautiful Montaukett Indian, prepared his regalia for ceremony. His regalia was woodland themed which reflected forest animals and wild flowers, made from Deer or buckskin, beaver, bear, turkey or racoon.

Wunnetunia made Tatoson's clothes by hand. She tanned the animal skin. Tanning is a process that would turn the animal skin into leather, which would last a long time. She would then cut and sew the leather piece of clothing into a breechcloth. Tatoson's breechcloth was decorated with the woodland theme, out of porcupine quills with matching leggings and moccasins.

Now dressed, Tatoson walked excitedly down the path towards the sacred Circle. He walked right into the strong but loving embrace of his Grandmother, Nu`pi Nuqut. She was standing at the entrance of the sacred circle to welcome all friends and family members to her Ancestral lands to celebrate the harvest festival.

She hugged Tatoson tight and whispered in his ear, "Grandson of mine, you are growing so fast! I'm so proud of you My Tatoson"! He gave Grandmother a quick smile and hug and Escaped her loving embrace and ran to meet his Uncles in the circle. He stood quietly and showed his respect as he waited for his Uncles to open with prayers.

They began asking the Creator to please bless the sacred Circle with an offering of tobacco. His Uncles prayed "God of the Winds, of the Sun, of the Fire, and of the Corn, of Earth, of the Sea, of Day, of Night, all the Four Seasons, we honor thee. The Uncles offered up tobacco an offering of the Old

Ways of Their ancestors. Next they began Smudging.
Smudging shows the Creator we are entering the sacred circle
With a good heart. Free from negativity and bad spirits.
The feather of an Eagle is used in smudging which symbolizes
the spiritual eagle bringing our prayers to the Creator.
Tatoson gets smudged and stands by the entrance to the circle,
for when prayers are completed dancing commences.
With prayers of honor and thanks now complete, the
Welcome Dance Begins.

Tatoson loves to dance! He loves the beat of
the drum and the feel of the Earth beneath his feet.
Dance is also considered a prayer not just a performance.

Next was the Medicine Dance, Tatoson ran and took a seat
upon his blanket and watched his Uncles dance. His older
cousins were next, they were Grass Dancers. He watched and
listened intently. He whispered out loud but to himself "I'm
going to be a Grass Dancer". He continued watching the
dancing, enjoying the Drummers. Next came the Shawl Dance,
Tatoson watched his Mother dance, he thought she was so
beautiful! He then watched
The Honor Dance and knew what was coming up next!

Tatoson folded up his blanket as he walked down the hill. He stopped to see his Mother and his Aunts all starting to prepare the feast. He got caught up in the yummy aromas of the Nunowa feast, it made his tummy rumble! He began looking into all the pots cooking on the open fire.

He then walked Over to one of the tables. Something smelled really good over there! All of a sudden he heard his Mother's voice. "Tatoson! "You are too big to be so underfoot! Go! Go watch your Uncles compete in their games of skill." Tatoson grabbed a piece of fry bread from the table before his Mother could half-heartedly swat his hand away! He kissed his Mother and ran.

Tatoson took a seat on an old tree stump. Here the men gathered, setting up for the games of skill and contests, that were soon to begin. The Uncles tested their skills of archery, target shooting, with counting games and seeking games. They played the day away. But Tatoson became such a distraction during the tomahawk toss, that the blade of one of the hawks came closer to him than the intended target! His Uncles exclaimed! "Tatoson! You are too young for such a toss!

You are underfoot, go now, go listen to the Grandmothers".

Tatoson thought to himself, as he walked back up the hill towards the Grandmothers, "too old to be in the kitchen, too young for the contests, oh... but wait! I am never too young or too old for Storytelling!" and he ran to the storytelling circle. He found the Grandmothers and his cousins gathering in the circle.

Tatoson sat close to his Grandmother Nu`pi Nuqut. He was excited to hear her storytelling. He always enjoys hearing her stories so much. She was the Eldest and wisest person he has ever known, and with the best stories!

We think of storytelling in all ways, through Music, Art, Reading, and Writing. But we also told stories in the simplest ways with Storytelling Beads. Tatoson enjoyed listening to the Grandmothers, each telling their own Story using colorful seeds and corn.

While the story was being told, Grandmother would touch the colored seeds and corn one by one as the story progressed.

Showing a visual representation to the verbal story spoken. It felt Almost like turning a page in a book. In honor of the harvest festival the Grandmothers storytelling is all about the fall season.

The necklaces honor Mother Earth.

Grandmother N`aham of the Turkey Clan shared, The Colors of Indian Corn.

To make these story necklaces Grandmother had to shuck corn and collect the pretty kernels in a bowl. She soaked them for a day or two to make them soft enough to work with. When they became nice and soft she took a threaded needle and using a wooden board pressed the seeds along the thread.

Grandmother N`aham began her story with her necklace.

"Mother Nature paints colors for you and me On all the Indian Corn that we see. Brown is for beauty that welcomes the Fall. Red is Mother Nature's love for us all. Yellow is the golden sun.

White reminds us to be kind to everyone. Orange tells us to be thankful each day for the variety of Nature and its wondrous ways.

Tatosons' colors of Indian corn story necklace were so wonderfully rich and earthly it reminded him of Autumn's Bounty. He was happy to wear it for the day.

Suddenly Grandmother Nunauk of the Wolf Clan

held up her story necklace and started signing!

"Hi Yah, Yah Ay! Hi Yah, Yah Ay!

All the cousins with Tatoson joined in the song!

They were so excited! Grandmother had a story necklace

for their favorite song! They all sang together!

"Fly like the eagle, run like the deer

Swim like fish, growl like the bear.

Slither like the snake, Creep like a fox.

Hop like the rabbit, prowl like the wolf.

Twinkle like the star, shine like the sun.

Blow like the wind, grow like a flower.

Flow like the mountain stream, turn

like the earth. Rumble like the thunder,

fall like the rain."

This song was a Pow wow song, it celebrates Fall.

The story celebrates animals and many wonders of Mother
Earth.

Tatosons' necklace of colored pumpkin seeds celebrates the

Animals and the bounty of nature.

To prepare for the Pow wow story necklace

Grandmother Nunauk made dyes from different native plants.

These furnished various tints as brown, red, green, blue, yellow,

Orange, and purple. Some of the native plants used to produce

These colored dyes were yarrow, sassafras and chokecherry.

CHAPTER THREE

"Story Necklaces"

Native American Necklaces have a long and interesting History of storytelling. These beads help tell stories of the past, and are handed down from generation to generation.

Traditionally, the Grandmothers, the Elders of the tribe used the story necklaces to explain the history of the tribe. They would explain what each bead meant and how it was used to the younger family members.

The storytellers when talking with the children would show them each colored bead as they tell the story. Many times there was no real story and the Grandmothers made up the story as they went and made the colored beads fit their story! The children enjoyed the stories so much!

The Grandmothers would get the squash seeds from the Seed Keeper. (An Elder who was gifted with great knowledge of their agricultural heritage). Their seeds spoke of stories and legends and representing spirits. The Grandmother's story necklaces told of daily life, as well as their history.

This time-honored oral culture passes traditional values and beliefs from one generation to the next.

Tatosons' Grandmother's seeds, corn and shell beads were incorporated to tell of history, legends and of their daily life too.

CHAPTER FOUR

"Nu`pi Nuqut"

All the cousins settled down close to Tatoson,
they all wanted to hear his Grandmother's Necklace story.
Nu`pi Nuqut was the eldest, wisest and most traditional
member of the Turtle Clan. She represented her Grandmother's
way of telling stories by gathering everyone around. Storytelling
was her Grandmother's Way of passing down tribal history.
She used different seeds and shell beads in succession to
portray different events.

Nu`pi Nuqut's Grandmother was a Squaw of great renown.
She had given her story necklaces to Warriors of her clan to
commemorate their deeds in hunting and in battle. These were
sacred and held in the highest regard. Nu`pi Nuqut's story
necklaces were designed to represent ancestors, animals, and
spirits. They illustrated history and legends, they were apart
of tribal life.

Tatosons' Grandmother's story necklaces like her
Grandmother's kept their culture alive. She celebrates
Nunowa with a story necklace that is traditional and honors the
Earth Mother.

She began her story;" Good happens when we share our
Stories and traditions surrounded by seeds, so I share with you
Today an old traditional one of long ago."

"We are part of a circle, the circle is large and full of life.
Creator created Creation for each of us. The circle of creation
is where we live. The earth is our Mother, and all is connected
to the earth. The earth has been given a mission and the
mission is to sustain life.

We must not become careless in our actions and
thoughts. Not giving Mother Earth much thought.
For when we do Earth Mother's heart becomes weak.
She will groan because of our thoughtless actions.
We are called to live in harmony and with respect for
creation and all our relations that share this sacred
space. When we are mindful of our actions and walk on this
earth with respect and humility, then we heal Our Mother
Earth."

Tatoson continued to listen and watch his Grandmother
intently as she continued her story necklace.
His Grandmother continued "this is my most favorite necklace
it's an old traditional one. It is made from materials found in

nature. The tribes of long ago that lived near the shore used shells and those in the forested areas would use seeds. Each tribe developed its own traditional stories with their colored seed beads and the stories were passed from one generation to the next."

Grandmother held up her necklace for everyone to see, as she explained; "my necklace is of seven beads. They represent the letters in the word "B.a.l.a.n.c.e" and are symbolic of living a life in harmony with Mother Earth. To walk in silence, walk in unison with Mother Earth's cycles. Listen to her wisdom. For all life is sacred and we are all related and this shall be passed down to the next seven generations. Walk in balance with Mother Earth. Honor the balance of life."

Grandmother lowered her necklace and began to add more of her story to it. She said "celebrating the circle of life, I add to my story necklace sunflower seeds, pumpkin seeds, fruit seeds, sea shells, and animal bone.

For my Grandmothers were from both the forests and the shores and always lived in balance with Mother Earth and each other".

Tatoson was so proud of his Grandmother and found
it such an honor to be able to put on his Grandmother's story
necklace. He was proud to be of the Turtle Clan and respected
his family so much.

He knew he would one day follow in his Uncle's footsteps,
working upon the bay and respecting Mother Earth and her
wondrous ways.

CHAPTER FIVE

"The Feast"

It was now time for the feast! Tatoson was getting hungry! He walked over to the Nunowa table looking at all they were about to dine on. He saw, the three sisters, of corn, beans, and squash. Oh and a vegetable dish called Succotash. There were some nuts and berries sitting next to some small loaves of cornbread. Both hot and some cold. He continued to eye the delicious table! There was fry bread and corn chowder, oh yum he thought! Wow, pumpkin, lobster, mussels too. Fish, some venison, duck and goose too

"Tatoson" Mother whispered in his ear, "now Tatoson you know to take your place beside your Uncles for prayer, now off you go!" as she gave him a gentle push away from the food.

Tatoson took his place beside his Uncles, and stood with respect. Uncle hid a smile and whispered to his Nephew, "prayers of thanks, then we feast" he said with a wink. Tatoson's smile went wide. He just knew his Uncles were as hungry as he!

Tatoson looked around the Nunowa feast. He saw his

Parents, Siblings, Grandparents, too. Aunts, Uncles, with his

cousins too. All his Turtle Clan, tribal family. Turkey, Wolf Clans,

friends too. Tatoson thought to himself, how he loves Nunowa.

Traditions shared with tribal family. Gathering together to

share prayers and a good meal. He was proud of his culture.

    Tatoson was finding his place in the clan.

    Tatoson asked if could end Nunowa with a prayer.

The Uncles all looked up at once! All eyes were on

Grandmother. She gave the Uncles a slight nod. They gave

Tatoson their blessing.

    Tatoson walked to the sacred circle, he felt all eyes on him

and it was suddenly quiet. But he was not nervous at all! He felt

so very proud!

He began;

  "The Earth is our Mother

Given to us by the Creator

To care for, not own

If we take care of the

Land, the land will take care

Of us. Protect her waters,

Air, soil, forests, plants,

And animals.

We thank you Mother Earth

For producing this food

And we thank all those who

Labored to bring it to us.

All responded A'hoy! Some clapped, his Uncles smiled, his Grandmother stood up and smiled with such a look of love and pride on her face.

Tatoson felt it and he smiled back. He just learned the true meaning of Nunowa.

Conclusion

"Nunowa Today"

Today, the descendants of Tatoson still observe this custom every Autumn and return to the land of their Ancestors and gather for the feast of Nunowa, all tribal family members and friends of the Wolf, Turkey and Turtle Clans contribute and prepare for a communal dinner. Everyone celebrating with traditional drumming, dancing, and tobacco offerings.

I and my family members the descendants of Tatoson still practice this ceremony, along with ancient rites and rituals of spirituality today so not to forget the old ways. People think we do not exist because we do not live on a reservation. But we are still here! Our ceremonies preserve our culture and we pass it on.

Documentation

"Indian Children"

BY: Annette Wynne 1919

"Pow Wow Song"

BY: Ben Hardaway

"The Colors of Indian Corn"

BY: Alina Thomas

"The Journey: Stories and Prayers"

From People of the First Nation

BY: Joyce Carison 1991

"Family Oral Stories"

Waters Family Little Neck NY

Vocabulary

Tatoson: ("He passed by")

Qunneke: ("A Doe")

Aunan: ("A Fawn")

Nuckqusha: ("I Fear Him")

Wunnetu Nia: ("My Heart is true")

Cowauontam: ("You Are a Wise Man")

Nupi Nuqut: ("Water Woman")

Weekan: ("It is Sweet")

Cowenaweke: ("You are a rich man")

Mishquock: ("Red Earth")

Wauompeg: ("White Wampum")

Cowauontam: ("You are a wise man")

Mapvanesto: ("Standing Waters")

CPSIA information can be obtained
at www.ICGtesting.com
Printed in the USA
BVHW041808180723
667438BV00004B/44

9 781987 551204